CONTENTS

A Quick Favor

I greatly appreciate your reading of this book- I've had a lot of fun writing it. I believe its content can help many people find the best accounting career path for themselves.

If you find this book valuable and interesting, it would mean a lot to me if you left a positive review, reflecting on your experience.

Click here -> Link to Amazon

You can also join my newsletter and receive several valuable, free gifts here-> Link

INTRODUCTION- GSD RECAP:

Getting Shit Done tackles a common yet daunting question; Why do organizations struggle to achieve their plans on time and on budget, AND what needs to change to ensure we meet our goals?

The challenge is very real, and the rewards are also high.

Here's what we know- Each year, organizations go through the same ritual where executive teams design their strategy and then pass it down through their organizations (a la whisper-down-the-lane) to be translated and implemented by the workers. But we all see and know that something gets lost in the middle between creating the plan (strategy) and carrying it out (execution).

Most people don't plan to fail, but a lack of understanding finds organizations inevitably falling back into the same trap over and over again. Researchers have long acknowledged that even the most brilliant strategy is worthless if it isn't executed well.

> *"Companies, on average, only deliver 63% of the financial performance on their strategies promise."-Harvard Business Review*
>
> *82% of Fortune 500 CEOs feel their organization is effective at strategic planning. Only 14% indicated to be effective at implementing the strategy."-Forbes Magazine*
>
> *Executional Excellence is the number one challenge facing global corporate leaders."-Harvard Business Review*

Slow strategy execution is the top challenge for 2019; 70% of executives say they had little confidence in their ability to solve the problem."-Gartner

50% of well-formulated strategies fail to deliver expected results because of poor execution."-Harvard Business Review "Only 2% of leaders feel confident that 80-100% of their goals will be executed."- Bridges Business Consultancy

Although organizations and industries can identify what needs to change, most strategy-execution efforts aren't successful. Those strategy executions that don't fail outright limp forward until the plug is pulled. Staggering price tags, incomplete deliverables, and a demoralized workforce usually lie in the wake of many change efforts.

Not that strategy-execution is a new problem, but the pace of competition and innovation today has substantially raised the stakes of the game. What worked yesterday may not work today, and an organization needs to be dynamic enough to choose new courses of action and make them a reality.

Enough already! Let's each take ownership of our roles, teams, and organizations so we thoroughly understand the strategy-execution gap, define what must change, and then make it happen.

CLOSING THE STRATEGY-EXECUTION GAP

Once the right strategy is in place, the focus shifts entirely to execution.

More than mere tactics, execution is the fundamental bridge between strategy and performance. It must be approached as a systematic process for rigorously reviewing and challenging strategic imperatives, operational directives, underlying capabilities, accountabilities, and performance outcomes.

Closing the strategy execution gap starts by acknowledging that execution is a distinctive discipline and skill set built over time. By learning how to set better targets, align resources, lead at all levels, deliver results, and build controls around processes, we learn to build a system that ensures what gets done stays done.

When managed as a disciplined process, strategy-execution is an iterative, adaptive, and robust method for running a business. Without this discipline — this systematic process — the strategy-execution lessons might remain only good ideas left sitting on a bookshelf.

While many managers and professionals may think of improving strategy-execution as identifying and removing the few, big, identifiable roadblocks like filling in a pothole in the middle of a highway, there is way more to it. Working towards strategy-execution is a multi-faceted process.

Like any discipline, strategy-execution depends on an earnest and wholehearted adoption, not choosing sections a la carte that fits best into your worldview. Each block builds upon the others to create a lasting structure.

Closing the strategy-execution gap is hard; really, really hard. Building a great organization, attracting, and retaining the right people, and building and maintaining excellence throughout an organization are challenges that can't be solved quickly. There is no simple color-by-numbers solution to fill in structural gaps for a prize so large in our organizations' health, profitability, and economies.

It is fair to go so far as to say that a lack of execution is one of the most significant problems facing businesses today. With it, you can overcome many deficiencies; without it, you're dead. Understanding and bridging the strategy-execution gap up to this point has been an ambiguous and murky exercise.

It isn't one thing or three things that we must get right once. Strategy-Execution is about all of us, executives, directors, managers, and employees getting the critical elements right all the time.

Strategy-Execution Questions

Getting Shit Done was written around exploring 12 key questions.

The three core questions of GSD:

1. Who will do the work?
2. What work needs to be done?
3. When will the work be done?

Supporting questions of GSD:

4. Who owns the problem, and who owns the solution?
5. Why isn't the work getting done?
6. Why isn't the work getting done on time?
7. Does each person in the organization understand What needs to be done?
8. Does each person understand How the work will be done?
9. Are we communicating as effectively and efficiently as possible to facilitate excellence?
10. Are you learning like a leader?
11. Are you thinking like a leader?
12. Are you executing like a leader?

However, the journey does not stop here. We must continue asking, assessing, understanding, improving, and repeating until the gap is closed.

This book greatly expands on the questions and the reflections at the end of each original chapter to assess where you and your organization stand concerning these principles.

265 Strategy-Execution Questions has been written to reinforce the critical points and consideration from each chapter of Getting Shit Done you can use to improve your skill set, team, function, and organization.

What causes the strategy-execution gap?

Years of compounded neglect and unintentionality in an organization often drives the strategy-execution gap. Organizational decay is like sand caught in many gears, which eventually causes a machine to sputter out of control. Unless you specifically look for the damage, the destruction can almost be unseen until it is too late. Likewise, by the time organizations acknowledge a strategy-execution issue, the cost of repairs is unmanageable.

According to the Harvard Business Review Advisory Council, senior executives wholeheartedly agree that an organization's architecture — which includes the very structures, processes, and systems supposed to enable work — is their most significant obstacle to strategic execution.

Obvious quick fixes are not the remedy- we must look deeper.

To Get Shit Done (and get it done right), combine the thirteen strategy-execution elements presented in the framework and in this book to create a powerful synergy and help you find best practices that work for your organization.

Without a clear framework, organizations are left to guesswork to fill in the strategy-execution gap that spans from expectations to deliverables. Add it all up, and the conclusion seems to be obvious:

1) Execution is essential both strategically and operationally,
2) Regardless of industry sector, we need to be better at it, and
3) Poor execution is a leading cause for concern among organizations.

When we are supported by an integrated, organization-wide framework that entails establishing the required strategies for success, we have a much greater chance of effectively executing those strategies.

	--	
1	Strategy	
2	Planning	
3	Focus	
4	Decentralization	
5	Ownership & Accountability	**Who**
6	Communication	**Will**
7	Culture	**Do**
8	Leadership	**What**
9	Experience	**and**
10	Skills	**By**
11	Professionalism	**When?**
12	Continuous Improvement Mindset	
13	Execution	
	--	

As Larry Bossidy explained in Execution, "Strategy-execution is an unending process that requires constant attention."

We now understand that goals are only met by embracing an intentional and systematic strategy-execution framework, not a patchwork of tools and policies to close the strategy-execution gap.

CH 1- GETTING SHIT DONE: THE STRATEGY-EXECUTION GAP

Takeaways

- An organization must embrace a unique strategy that serves a need in the overall market that competitors cannot copy.
- Strategy is choosing what to do and what not to do. All strategies boil down to 1 of 2 alternatives:
    - Do what everyone else is doing (but spend less money doing it), or
    - Do something no one else can do.
- Executing strategy is circular and continuous, not linear.
- Organizations must find a way to be great at setting the strategy and sustaining core competencies with a long-term perspective.
- An organization requires a core set of competencies that make achieving the strategy possible in the short and long term. It's not enough to get one or two competencies right- Linkage between core competencies and strategy is crucial to forging Fit.
- Fit occurs when the strategy and core competencies are aligned.
- Fit is extremely difficult for competitors to imitate and is the path to sustainable long-term profitability. The fit premium reflects the reality that distinctive capabilities are:
    - Difficult to build
    - Complex and high value
    - High fixed costs in human capital, tools, and systems.
- The strategy-execution gap is the disconnect between a strategy being set and people closest to the work knowing what the strategy is and what they must do to help achieve it.
- There is no good strategy and failed implementation.

The strategy is flawed if an organization is not aware of its core capabilities and limitations and moves forward anyway.

- What worked yesterday may not work today, and an organization must be dynamic enough to choose new courses of action and make them a reality.
- Although organizations and industries can identify what needs to change, most strategy-execution efforts fail. The discipline of strategy-execution must be mastered to close the strategy-execution gap.
- If your "strategy" only communicates what you hope the outcome will be but not what you will do, it doesn't work.
- Not only must an organization know where it wants to go, but it must also have the capabilities, functions, and people in place to help it get there.
- In today's fast-paced business world, the difference between great and not-so-great companies comes down to their ability to execute the best strategic plan.

Questions

Build the strategy:

13. Does the organization understand and articulate how they add value for customers that others don't?
14. Is the customer identified, and is it understood why they buy from you?
15. How are our customer needs changing? What might they want different or better in the future?
16. Does the strategy create customer value that is difficult for competitors to replicate?
17. To what degree are offerings clearly differentiated in their market?
18. How much ease and expense are required for your customer to switch to a competitor's offering?
19. How well do the organization's products solve the customers' problems and meet their expectations?
20. How aligned are your organization's offerings to meet market demand?
21. Are strategy assumptions accurate and relevant?
22. Is the plan overly complex, or is it practical and straightforward?
23. Are changes in the competitive landscape identified, discussed, and tied into the most current strategy?
24. Does your organization regularly assess its strengths, weaknesses, opportunities, and threats to understand the current business climate?
25. Does your organization analyze the competition to understand competitive advantages and disadvantages and identify areas for investment or needs for improvement?
26. Does your organization strategically differentiate from the competition in terms of the capabilities of its product? How clear is your organization's strategy for this?
27. Does the organization have a current view of the competitive landscape and understand where they

fit into it?

28. What could disrupt the organization and render the strategy worthless?
29. What are the critical few business goals of the organization?
30. What are the specific desired outcomes of the strategy?
31. Do leaders across the organization believe the strategy will be practical and realistic to create long-term value?
32. Does the organization agree and stick to core businesses and opportunities? Do they agree with what they will say no to?
33. Are the right people involved in building and communicating the strategy?
34. Does the organization invite a diverse employee group into the strategy-setting meetings to provide feedback and insights?
35. Does the strategy have buy-in from key stakeholders?
36. Has the budget and funding been made available to invest in making the strategy a reality? Are contingency plans and risk assessment budgeted for?
37. Is the strategy realistic given the available timeline, resources, people, and budget?
38. Do key stakeholders continue to disagree on strategy, priorities, resources, funding, or timing? Have dissenters been silenced by being pushed out without having legitimate concerns heard and addressed?

Building Core Competencies

39. Does the organization first "build the strategy, then think about execution?" Or does it ask, "What capabilities are required to execute the strategy?" Don't assume execution is a given.
40. Do all people in the organization understand the strategy and their role in it?
41. Does the organization understand its core competencies and deficiencies?
42. What specific core operational capabilities enable your organization to excel at that value proposition? What 3-6 things do you do better than your competitors?
43. What activities must be eliminated, outsourced, or cut so that the company can focus on what it does best?
44. Does the organization enable employees to work together across organizational silos to tackle the cross-functional challenges that will allow the company to win?
45. Does the organization keep track of performance and how its building and scaling up those few key capabilities to create value for customers in ways that others cannot?
46. Is your whole management team engaged in building and executing the strategy—not just by measuring results but by continually challenging the organization and supporting it in improving its key capabilities? Do you set your team's sights high enough for what they must accomplish, and by when?
47. Has the organization identified the people vital to executing the strategy and ensuring they stick around by being compensated/recognized/rewarded appropriately?

48. Are there defined programs (for example, specific new technologies, new processes, or training programs) to further build your organization's critical capabilities to win with its strategy?
49. Have pet projects and legacy functions been identified, and has a remediation plan been put in place to dislodge them?
50. Does the organization understand and have a realistic plan for building or reinforcing the most important new or existing capabilities?
51. Which existing processes or functions hinder strategy-execution?
52. Does the organization understand its operational strengths, weaknesses, and opportunities?
53. Does the organization have the people and capability to build/strengthen core competencies internally, or are external resources also required? If external resources are needed, is there a budget available?
54. Does the organization have a way to determine if its efforts toward building core capabilities are on track?
55. Does your organization utilize its people as an asset to help it improve, stay competitive, and strategically meet goals? Are people used efficiently, or is talent wasted due to a lack of effective strategy?
56. Does your organization pursue growth and new businesses/market development with as much passion as it does operational efficiency?
57. Does your organization promote itself through its people? Do the people actively promote your organization?
58. Do you have a long-term vision of the innovations you will need to sustain the enterprise's core capabilities?

Forging Fit:

59. Does the organization understand and possess the capabilities required to achieve the strategy? Who is responsible for maintaining and enhancing the core capabilities?
60. Are you very clear about the specific capabilities that enable you to excel at that value proposition?
61. Have the underlying processes, systems, skills, and structures critical to driving performance for each capability been identified?
62. Which core capabilities drive the most value to customers?
63. Can competitors quickly replicate strategy and core competencies, or does a unique and sustainable opportunity exist?
64. Are resources available to forge fit? Do employees have the training, budget, and time available to reinforce the most valuable activities?
65. Does the organization understand the hurdles that inhibit fit? Is there a realistic plan to address them?
66. Does the organization understand what activities/functions/business units need to be eliminated to strengthen fit?
67. What, if anything, needs to change to make strategy-execution & fit realistic and attainable?
68. Is there a plan for how to improve the balance between core capabilities and strategic objectives over time?
69. Does your organization maximize existing resources to deliver the product offering?
70. How do you know that you have organizational alignment in core areas? When do you know your systems are misaligned?
71. Does the organization have a measure/gauge/system

to assess when fit diminishes? If so, who is responsible for strengthening fit?

72. Do stealth initiatives and executive "pet" projects bypass the core planning function? Are these being discussed and addressed/
73. Does the organization keep track of how its building and scaling up key capabilities enable value creation for customers in ways others cannot?
74. What must change, and what must stay the same?

CH 2- WHY SHIT DOESN'T GET DONE ON TIME

Takeaways

- No implementation can save a strategy that is not feasible or sound to begin with.
- Strategy is often poisoned at the planning level. When there are too many projects with fuzzy deadlines, resources, and ownership assignments, execution becomes unrealistic.
- Stuff doesn't get done because we often have inadequate planning, adjusting, and replanning systems. Stop strategic planning. Commit to strategic management.
- Planning is essential, but the goal isn't to create a plan. The goal is to develop and sustain a clear, concise, clear focus, execute it effectively, and do it repeatedly.
- Address the Planning Fallacy but understand our tendency to properly consider how long past projects have taken and assume that challenges/delays won't occur. Build-in allowances using simple tools like the EUR ratio that applies an allowance factor utilizing group experiences.
- To improve organizational efficacy in strategy-execution, people must exhibit ownership over their time, priorities, and output.
- Understand where your time goes to understand what could change to reduce time spent on non-value-added activities. Build the discipline to your routine to safeguard against the time you do have.
- Without a more thoughtful and conscientious approach to work, we leave too much to chance. We often have a "take it as it comes mentality" without much awareness.
    - We bend to the circumstances around us.
    - We let other people's poor attitudes and habits deter us.
    - We let our environment dictate how we

approach our work and our degree of ownership.

- We also confuse being busy with being productive.

- Managing time creates the freedom to work creatively by prioritizing and systemizing communication to increase the available time. Take control of time and focus. Review the tasks that must be completed and complete those that add to the organization's most significant impact. Guard your time like it is the most important asset you have.
- Focus on the essential matters. As you begin each day, ask what important issues are being put aside for trivial issues that seem urgent. Focus on your vital contribution first, not around the edges of trivial issues. Apply the 80/20 Rule- Pareto Principle to identify the key priorities and apply available resources to the tasks or projects that will yield the most significant benefits.
- We don't get stuff done on time because we are too distracted. Commit to Being 100% present on critical work. Don't allow yourself to become distracted, and allow circumstances to dictate how your time is spent. Stay un-distracted. Turn off all "push" notifications on your phone and computer.
- To produce high-quality work consistently, we must allocate large blocks of time undistracted and focused. Create, experiment, and hone a system that allows you to take back ownership of your time to enhance your productivity.
- To demonstrate leadership in your organization by achieving a Sense of Urgency, focus on communicating with energy and passion. Speaking with power and purpose is vital towards inspiring others to act.
- Use tools like the Eisenhower Box to categorize and prioritize work into 4 categories that determine whether the task should be done immediately, a

decision promptly made, or otherwise delegated or deleted.

Questions

75. When plans or strategies are communicated, are the assumptions and targets compared to the available resources to determine if a strategy is feasible?
76. Does the organization cascade strategic objectives to individual goals and targets while identifying internal dependencies and timelines to achieve this goal?
77. Are you effectively motivating others and focusing/leveraging organizational energy by instilling a Sense of Urgency?
78. Do people understand which tasks or work can or should be delegated to someone else to allow more time to focus on the big picture and keep the pieces aligned and moving?
79. Is alignment established on who is working on which strategic objective?
80. Does the organization set & communicate the specific objectives that must be achieved? Is there a process or framework for updating the metrics?
81. Are early indicators in place to signal if something isn't working or hitting the desired targets? Are there plans in place for correcting any potential issues?
82. Do people focus on the 20% of things that matter, or do they approach everything with the same level of prioritization?
83. Is analysis done to understand how much time and energy is spent on various tasks and workstreams?
84. Do employees complete tasks at the last minute or frequently ask for extensions? Is a root-cause analysis performed and issued addressed?
85. Is time for planning and scheduling built into the daily routines? Does a daily huddle occur where team members commit to achieving x during the day, and are those goals/progress reviewed the following day?

86. Are to-do Lists or action lists discussed and aligned? Are priorities discussed and confirmed with managers and coworkers? Do workers set daily, weekly, and monthly targets and continuously assess performance against those targets?
87. Is short, mid, and long-term goal setting used to decide which tasks and activities will be worked on?
88. Do plans allow for contingency time to deal with "the unexpected"?
89. Are unexpected issues analyzed, categorized, escalated, and dealt with?
90. Do employees understand whether tasks they are working on are high, medium, or low value?
91. Are expectations clearly set with others? Do others respect these commitments?
92. When new assignments are given, is analysis completed to analyze the importance and prioritize it accordingly?
93. Are employees encouraged and empowered to do work that adds value and optimize/automate/eliminate low-value work?
94. Are workers routinely stressed about deadlines and commitments? Do employees take work home to get it done?
95. Is the workplace designed to minimize distractions and enable deep work? For example, are meetings discouraged on certain days?
96. Is there a history of not getting things done on time? Are the root causes understood and discussed?
97. Do people throughout the organization diligently follow through on what you have decided? Is backtracking or digressing tolerated and accepted?
98. Has the organization adopted formal/informal policies to free up available time? Have wasteful activities been identified and discouraged?
99. Are distractions permitted to enter your world and

steal your time? Review your phone and computer settings and set them so that you decide when to engage with them.

CH 3- PUSH DOWN THE POWER: AUTONOMY, EMPOWERMENT, AND DECENTRALIZATION

Takeaways

- In addition to an overall direction supporting a primary strategy known as the Big What, a successful strategy also requires several secondary strategies that must be autonomously and simultaneously set and executed by people at all levels of the organization.
    - The Big What= The primary strategy/vision
    - The Little Whats= Supporting competencies/ execution
- The Little Whats gives people the time and practice they need to turn from amateurs to true professionals. These are known as the Little Whats.
- The Little Whats is about setting expectations around continuously developing our execution muscles by improving the organization's work. The critical core competencies can be built, maintained, and improved by demanding excellence and autonomy from each person in each function throughout the organization.
- The Little Whats has two elements to it:
    - People must be empowered to do great work within their zone of influence as efficiently, error-free, and cost-effective as possible and be rewarded for it.
    - Company leadership should have minimal/ no decision-making power in how people accomplish their tasks in their areas of expertise.
- To close the strategy-execution gap, getting the big things right means getting the small things right first. If departments, functions, and processes aren't optimized, fit between the Big What and Little What will not be found, and the strategy-execution gap will persist.

- Rules and hierarchies are often implemented to mitigate the risk of facing alternative courses of action. While harmless as a concept, they are often disastrous in practice and result in having the opposite outcome desired.
- To provide direction and strategic objectives, use the concept of Commander's Intent and decentralization to communicate the objectives and build cohesion.
- Commander's Intent teaches us that the ultimate goal is to help people make good decisions. Ownership and accountability are core tenets that make for a happier & more agile workforce high in engagement and deadly in execution.
- Establishing Commander's Intent in your organization focuses on people and empowers them. Instead of using rules, Commanders Intent is communicated through guidelines. Getting things done through others is a fundamental leadership skill.
    - "Here's what we think is right in most circumstances but do what's in the company's best interest. Do the right thing."
    - Commander's Intent broadcasts this message: "We have problem X, and I trust you to solve it." It doesn't matter, within means, which paths are explored or ultimately taken to solve a problem, so long as it is solved.
- Focus people around one rule," Do the right thing." Then, give people the tools and support they need to identify and solve the problems. Give your people every opportunity and means to meet those goals. Get out of their way. Focus on simplistic and common-sense approaches towards aligning others and measuring results. Good judgment is hard to define and harder still to acquire. Judgment can be improved with practice.
- Establish a strong Commander's Intent within the organization and a bottom-

up hierarchy. Decentralization & empowerment are essential for helping others develop critical thinking skills and mastery. Hire the best people and empower them. Don't tell people what they can and can't do; tell them to do the right thing and let them decide for themselves. If employees need a step-by-step explanation of the right thing, they're not the right person. Teach them how to be responsible and accountable for executing their own to develop a creative, diligent, and solution-oriented team because they don't need to wait for your approval to implement when they're ready.

- Trusting a larger group of people closest to the work to find the best solution allows more ideas to come to the table. The person closest to the work has the best and most timely information and is best suited to act. Decentralization makes strategy-execution possible.
- When people are granted autonomy, they feel empowered in their roles and responsible for their actions and their organization's success. Instead of roadblocks demoralizing the workforce, workers are energized by the opportunity to demonstrate their mastery in overcoming challenges.
- Focus on realistic levels of errors and priorities. For example, the Pareto principle has proven that 20% of inputs control 80% of the outputs. Act on what matters.
- Set SMART expectations; Specific, Measurable, Attainable, Realistic, and Measurable to assess and keep strategy-execution on track.

Questions

100. Does your organization have a model or framework that guides your strategic planning and execution process? Is responsibility for results cascaded appropriately through all levels of the organization?

101. Is the strategy clearly and thoroughly communicated throughout the organization? Does each person understand how the big goals tie to their day-to-day?

102. Does each person understand what they must do each day to help the strategy succeed? Do leaders tie strategic objectives to their daily tasks?

103. Are ownership, accountability, and excellence a requirement for working at your organization? How is this level of mastery evaluated, measured, and improved upon?

104. Have autonomy, empowerment, and decentralization been discussed with managers and expectations clarified?

105. Do managers understand how to coach instead of dictating instructions to their teams?

106. Does the organization make coaching/ mentoring available to those who want and need it?

107. Does your organization promote individuals based on initiative and results or tenure? Time spent in a role at an organization does not qualify you as an owner. Hiring, recognition, and promotion must foster a culture of focus on job results, commitment, and growth.

108. Does the organization recognize improvements made by employees and publicly reward those efforts to reinforce the behaviors?

109. Are people trusted and empowered to

do the right thing and drive improvements in their work? Are they recognized and rewarded for doing so?

110. Does each person feel empowered to do their best work? Does the organization measure the degree of empowerment and remove the existing roadblocks? Is someone accountable for ensuring empowerment?

111. Do employees lack the ownership mindset to execute the strategy effectively? Is there a plan to bring these people onboard or coach them out?

112. Are employees empowered to take the appropriate action to execute the strategy? Do leaders provide the right level of guidance, support, and direction?

113. When errors and mistakes occur in good faith, does the organization learn from them, or do they reprimand those responsible and impair empowerment?

114. Has your organization taken steps to flatten the hierarchical management structure? Minimizing traditional organizational charts and special perks, like corner offices and fancy furniture, allows employees to feel more respected. If they feel equal, they will interact with leaders and become role models for better communication, recognition, and mentoring.

115. Do leaders have the tools and capabilities to review daily/weekly/monthly metrics with the desired level of detail?

116. Are metrics appropriately designed to drive accountability and change?

117. Are people recognized and celebrated for meeting or exceeding their targets?

118. Do the metrics reinforce strategy-execution by measuring and managing each aspect

of the business?

CH 4- OWNERSHIP & ACCOUNTABILITY

Takeaways

- For the last 100+ years, Taylorism and the Principles of Scientific Management have kept workers down by giving control and ownership to managers and owners to dictate how work was done and own the rewards/outcomes.
- Taylor recommended the rigorous separation of planning and execution.
    - Describing his methods with pride, Taylor proclaimed that:
    - "The work of every workman is fully planned out by management at least one day in advance," and
    - "Each man receives in most cases complete written instructions, describing in detail the task which he is to accomplish."
- The shortcomings of Taylorism are the following:
    - Managers do not have the resources or technical understanding to dictate how work is done. At the same time, work complexity has increased.
    - The less stable and dynamic the environment is, the more that specialist skills and expertise matter.
    - The individual initiative-taking and problem-solving skills required to overcome these obstacles are discouraged.
- Physical ownership and Taylorism don't work because they disengage workforces.
    - People value freedom, autonomy, and growth.
    - Worker experimentation and decision-making lead to higher knowledge and skill levels, and these activities are discouraged.
- Mental ownership is the key to the future. The idea of ownership can equally, perhaps more significantly, refer to the experience of being psychologically tied to an idea, an identity, or an entity.
- Mental Ownership works because it combines 1) employee

engagement and 2) ties them to outcomes. Unless employees have real incentives to implement the strategy, they will not commit to it, and the implementation will fail.

- Mental Ownership means you will 1) deliver as promised, respecting any deadlines or budget constraints mandated to you. It also means 2) you're forthcoming when, as sometimes happens, you couldn't deliver.
- Improvement is needed at all organizational levels for change to occur, top leadership, managers, and individuals. Ownership builds a collective mastery that is hard to duplicate.
- When employees take ownership of their work, they treat the business they are working for — and its money — as if it were their own. They will make decisions thoughtfully, responsibly, and with more care. They will also be more driven, motivated, and have more initiative, seeking creative and innovative ways to improve and develop what they are doing, rather than going through the motions and fulfilling the minimum, and worse still, stagnating.
- Taking ownership tells others — "You can trust me to do the right thing."
- When we think of accountability, we typically think of holding others accountable. But the most influential leaders and teammates are more focused on holding themselves accountable. The locus of control shifts from outside to inside by exhibiting ownership and accountability. From practice to intentions. From strategic to personal. Accountability needs to be at all levels of the company.
- Complaining is the voice of helplessness; Owners are accountable for reconstituting the world around them. Fix what's broken and champion for change. The expectation at work should be excellence.
- If there is any level of surprise when a deadline comes and goes and the work still has not been completed, then you're not an owner; you're a renter.

Questions

119. Do employees have an interest in helping the organization succeed? Are their interests tied to the organization in a meaningful way?

120. Is your organization doing its part to make the employees owners? Are stock and stock options issued to remove stakeholder conflicts of interest between employees and investors?

121. Are ownership and accountability expectations clear and outcomes definable for each person, team, and function?

122. Are the rewards and repercussions for succeeding (or not) clear and explicit?

123. Is Accountability Explicit? Are expectations clear and promises honored?

124. Who is accountable within the company for the execution of the strategy and the processes of implementation at the highest level? What about the remaining tiers? Are people tied to strategy-execution?

125. Are executives, managers, and employees all held accountable for delivering on their objectives by the promised date? How are misses and achievements addressed?

126. Does the organization tie in Who does What and by When to all strategic objectives, milestones, and objectives? Are people personally connected to ensuring success? Are there repercussions and rewards in place for outcomes?

127. Are people encouraged to bring an emotional commitment to their work and feel mutually accountable for results?

128. Are personal, team, function, and organizational accountability measured against targets and rewarded? Does the organization have a

plan to reinforce the right behaviors?

129. Are leaders setting the right example by acting as role models to do what they said they would do when promised? Are remediation plans communicated, if not?

130. Does the organization have a plan to address employees not interested in taking ownership of their work?

131. Does the organization have a plan to remediate poor performance?

132. Does the organization have a strategy-based performance management plan linked to individual development plans?

133. Are employees motivated every day to understand what they're doing and how it connects to the critical strategic levers?

134. Do people initially create their own strategic goals to capture their ambition and preference? Do managers work to align employees' goals with the larger strategic plan?

135. Is there a regular program to engage and empower the talent in the organization?

136. Are employees really given the power to make decisions?

137. If not you, then who?

138. If not now, then when?

139. Do you spend more time working or complaining?

140. Do you more often push forward or procrastinate?

141. Do you tend to point fingers or problem-solve?

142. What excuse(s) do you commonly use or hear to explain why work doesn't get done in your organization? What could be done to mitigate this?

143. Are you active in helping or hindering

efforts to establish an environment that accepts excuses?

144. Count the number of times you blamed Somebody else or an external circumstance and have actively looked for how you could solve the problem. What do you need to change in your demeanor to exhibit Extreme Ownership?

145. What can you do to help shift the locus of control from outside to inside, from practice to intentions, from the strategic to personal?

146. Where can you start to build accountability chains in your work, team, function, and organization?

147. What can be improved in terms of ownership and accountability? Where have you disappointed others, and what will you do to ensure it doesn't happen again?

148. How often have you thought, "that is not my job," in the past week or month? What were the results? What could you do to improve the outcomes next time?

149. How often are workers encouraged to build ownership and accountability chains by understanding the bigger picture of their work and how it connects to related tasks up and downstream?

150. How often do deadlines come and go without someone following up on a task? Do teammates step up, explain what happened, and how to prevent the issue from occurring again?

151. Do people support each other and build up the team instead of blaming and tearing each other down?

CH 5- GETTING SHIT DONE BY COMMUNICATING FOR EFFECTIVENESS

Takeaways

- Communication helps members understand the organization's strategy, why it is needed, its goals, and what must be done to succeed. Be clear, concise, and consistent with communication.
- Strategy-execution is all about acting and achieving results. Communication assigns responsibility for ensuring the Who, What, and When are apparent to each person throughout the organization. The message must reach all places at all times and mean the same thing to everyone.
- If the Why is not communicated along with Who Will do What and by When then the strategy-execution gap will persist.
- Poor communication is a vital factor that must be addressed in discussing work delays or botched strategy-execution. The fault may lie with either the message sender or the message receiver, but it doesn't matter: if one person is wrong, we're all wrong. Unless best practices are understood and adopted, miscommunication will keep occurring.
- Focus on using communication to build alignment where everyone is focused on the same strategic outcomes, with a shared understanding of their roles, commitment, and accountability to deliver exceptional performance.
- Use process-centric communication to avoid excessive steps that consume resources and time.
- The right message needs to be delivered in the right way. Understand how to communicate each message to different audiences best.
- Facilitating a two-way communication flow is the best way to get your employees on board with the strategy and vision. Explain the why to obtain buy-in.
    - Do they care?
    - Do employees internalize the ambitions of the organization into their values? Offer the

opportunity to ask people for specific examples of what support and additional information are required. And what they do not look like- this holds them accountable for asking for what they need.

- Balance using all communication channels instead of those most comfortable to meet the audience's needs. The objective needs to be clear, and accountability needs to be clear.
- Be accessible, speak often with your team about the challenges faced. Don't hide or discount the current reality of challenges and shortfalls.
- Be specific in communicating the vision and goals. Employees can't be owners if they don't understand the business targets and realities.
- Ask others for direct feedback on their understanding of the messages shared and ask for what can be improved or changed.
- Where possible, use process-centric communication to increase the speed and efficiency of sharing ideas while reducing the number of steps.
- To reduce or eliminate costly work delays, it is always a good idea to follow up with any communication effort to be sure that recipients have:
    - Received the message.
    - Understood the message.
    - Can articulate back to you Who will Do What and by When.

Questions

152. Do leaders share all the facts and figures that can and should be shared with employees? Is there a level of transparency and vulnerability?
153. Does leadership take the time to understand how well messages have been communicated and understood?
154. Are messages balanced to reach large audiences and individuals to emphasize impact and relevance?
155. Is there a plan or framework in place to communicate progress towards achieving the strategy?
156. Do organizational communication habits inhibit or accelerate progress?
157. Do you and those around you grasp the Why? Is there a connection between tasks and workstreams to the strategy?
158. Does the communication effectively identify the key messages for each segment of the population?
159. Has the organization identified ways to brand and simplify the strategy to make it memorable? Acronyms are a great tool here.
160. Does the organization have mechanisms in place to capture employee feedback throughout the strategy-execution journey?
161. Do discussions take place on why execution failures have occurred previously? Is there a plan to address these issues and gaps?
162. What or who will change to ensure that future failures don't persist?
163. Is strategy-execution discussed and reinforced at every available meeting?

164. Is the strategy explained to employees where they can tie their daily work to the goals and milestones?

165. What must be communicated differently to make people care about the strategy?

166. Do leaders at all levels appropriately explain why the organization must transform? Do they explain the positive and negative alternatives and outcomes?

167. Are goals cascaded down the org chart? Are they translated into individual expectations? Are measurement and reporting systems focused on the few big vital metrics that must be achieved?

168. Do leaders drive and champion strategy-execution? How?

169. Are individuals and leaders encouraged and rewarded for reinforcing Who does What and by When?

170. Does the organization find ways to share customer feedback (positive & negative) with the employees?

171. Does the organization find ways to share success stories from internal and external customers?

172. Does the organization layout the milestones that must be achieved for the strategy to be successful? Do they communicate when milestones are reached and recognize the key players?

173. Is a goal identified for communication? Are metrics or other measures in place to assess the effectiveness?

174. Does the organization recognize and set a plan for identifying and addressing the strengths and weaknesses in communication?

175. Do people have more or fewer questions

and concerns after group and organizational communication?

176. Does your organization clearly communicate the strategy, big picture, and current reality?

177. Is your communication efficient? Do you communicate in ways to shift the burden of completing the communication back to the sender?

178. Do you overuse acronyms and abbreviations that confuse others? Do you take the time to explain to others when they look confused?

179. Are you mindful in communication? Do you carefully consider the best channel and use of everyone's time?

180. Did you communicate why you needed to achieve them and how you intended to achieve them?

181. Does leadership reinforce communication best practices and remediate bottlenecks and frequent causes of miscommunication?

CH 6- INSTILL A GETTING SHIT DONE CULTURE

Takeaways

- Creating the proper organizational infrastructure allows companies to excel in their markets. Building and sustaining advantages is not just about winning today but building an engine for growth that will last long into the future.
- Culture is an essential component of strategy-execution that defines the organizational values and how people work together and communicate. Culture is ever-changing, and building it must be a mindful exercise to get good habits to stick.
- Ways of Working is vital because it helps an organization always remember that we must build alignment between culture and strategy.
- By setting an example, leaders, both past and present, can become guiding forces in aligning culture and strategy elements.
- One way to strengthen culture is through adopting Ways of Working, where each organization can set a unique code that conforms with its existing culture and desired results.
    - Once the organization's leadership decides the code, building Ways of Working into the organization involves tapping influential individuals with or without leadership titles to embrace these principles daily.
    - The next step is reinforcing shared values by recognizing and rewarding those who set exemplary examples.
    - Others will follow once it becomes evident that the organization is moving in a new direction, where rewards are shared based on what we do and how we do it.
    - Change then happens one interaction, one project, and one day at a time. If underlying assumptions are not challenged, understood, or identified

limitations, those responsible for execution will not bridge the gap between dreams and reality.

- Assumptions weaken strategy-execution. Guide the culture to deter assumptions:
  - Clarify strategy.
  - Clarify high-level strategy statements, separating and organizing goals, objectives, initiatives, aspirations, and strategies.
  - Create a transparent model that helps the organization understand the current strategies and differentiate them from operational improvements.
- Embrace conflict and candor to build alignment, resolve issues, and increase the level of trust and transparency. Take issues head-on, especially the uncomfortable ones. Confront reality, not the person. Don't bury your head in the sand.
- Alignment between strategy and core capabilities is critical to closing the strategy-execution gap. Strategy-execution is not a "one and done" effort. Over time, it grows from the compound effect of decisions, investments, and actions. Culture is a central ingredient to sustainably closing the strategy-execution gap.
- A culture that promotes small actions by lots of people will result in a significant change.
  - $1^{365} = 1$
  - $1.01^{365} = 37.7$!

182. Does the organization have a plan to make each function/team more effective and collaborative?
183. Does your culture optimize the implementation of your business model and strategy?
184. Do leaders enable the culture to achieve the stated value proposition?
185. Does the culture of your organization inhibit or enhance the organization? Can you answer: What Must Our Culture Look Like to Win?
186. Does your organization provide employee feedback and coaching in real-time? Can you describe specific behaviors that must change and provide your actual examples so the team member can "step into" the past scenarios?
187. Does the organization understand its unique Ways of Working? Are there unique ways of getting things done that are shared across the organization that strengthen it?
188. Does the organization reinforce the importance of building excellence in everyday activities? Are champions identified and rewarded?
189. How will the culture impact the changes required to build core competencies and find Fit?
190. Does misalignment exist because of assumptions, a lack of candor, and an aversion to conflict? If so, how can you change your behavior and influence others to improve the situation?
191. Does the culture prize and emphasize simplicity? Are employees encouraged or rewarded for removing unnecessary complexity?
192. Do leaders take time to assess, discuss,

and remediate what is working well versus not working well in the culture?

193. Do leaders understand which aspects of the organization's current culture influence and strengthen core capabilities?

194. Does the organization make it easy and straightforward for employees to bring up challenges they face? Is someone made responsible for removing these roadblocks?

195. Does the organization understand the strengths and weaknesses of its culture? Can the culture be described, and do the descriptions align across multiple perspectives?

196. Does the organization understand how the culture has enabled or inhibited past success?

197. Are a majority of employees and leaders engaged? If yes, how do you know? Are regular surveys, discussions, and assessments done to measure engagement?

198. Are major transformation efforts going too slow or stalled? Does the culture have a mechanism for recognizing these gaps and closing them?

199. Is there a cultural philosophy of continuous improvement in the planning and execution processes of the organization?

200. Does the culture enable employees to work together across organizational silos to tackle cross-functional challenges?

201. Are you setting a positive example to influence the culture?

202. What can you do to influence the culture in the right direction?

CH 7- GETTING SHIT DONE BY LEARNING LIKE A LEADER

Takeaways

- The Dunning-Kruger Effect- ignorance of one's ignorance.
    - We are not as good as we think —we frequently overestimate our ability and underestimate others' abilities. Low awareness + low cognitive ability= overestimation of capabilities
    - There is room to improve.
    - We must practice self-awareness by embracing humility and critical thinking. Businesses and individuals who challenge their assumptions will, at worst, come away better equipped to improve themselves and their processes.
    - "We are blind to our blindness." -Daniel Kahneman
    - "To transform an organization, you either have to change the people . . . or change the people." -Strategic Execution
- Grit
    - "No" isn't an option.
    - talent x effort = skill
    - All challenges can be overcome.
    - Adversity is a friend, not an enemy.
    - Grit begins with having an" ultimate concern"–a goal you care about so much that it organizes and gives meaning to almost everything you do. Grit is about sticking through tough times and obstacles and maintaining the same top-level goal for a very long time.
    - While we know what is good for us, we still struggle to be mindful enough to build up the

mental armor that keeps poor habits at bay when we're exhausted.

- Deliberate Practice
    - We only improve with a focused practice that stretches our capabilities.
    - We must regularly assess our skills and improve both strengths and weaknesses.
    - Knowledge + skill are required to bridge the gap between strategy and execution. (Knowledge + Skill = Capabilities)
    - The takeaway is that mastery can be attained by deliberately practicing a skill for long periods. To reach our goals, we must first change our lifestyle and daily habits to see changes (and results) later.
- Two Types of Intelligence
    - Fluid Intelligence
        - We are all born with fluid intelligence, which increases through adolescence and early adulthood. Fluid intelligence begins to decline gradually beginning in your 30s.
        - Capacity to reason
        - Ability to learn new things
        - Abstract thinking and problem-solving abilities
    - Crystallized Intelligence
        - Inversely, the crystallized intelligence curve goes up through your 30's 40's, 50's, and beyond well into advanced age.
        - Based on facts
        - Increases with age
        - Prior learning and experiences

- Most Training is Useless
    - Training connotes an experience that is a painful, time-consuming, and utterly useless exercise by most accounts, pretending to take employee development seriously. Outsiders teaching on subjects that are not applicable to work result in wasted time and money
    - The key is to assess the effectiveness of training offered in your organization by asking the following questions:
        - What behaviors must change to convince people that new skills, abilities, and capabilities are required?
        - Are the right people performing the training?
        - How will the impact of the training be measured? Who will perform the follow-ups?
        - What must happen before and after the training sessions occur to bring about change?

Questions

203. Ask yourself, "Did I sharpen my skills today?" Your skills might involve technical skills related to your job, or they might refer to your listening skills if you're looking to improve your communication. What new skills or knowledge have you been building on?

204. How effectively is your organization establishing the capacity to manage reasonable risk by trying new things, prototyping, testing, and learning?

205. How well does your team and organization share what you've learned with other parts of the organization?

206. Is the learning mindset a nice to have or a must-have at your organization? Has this led to positive results or dissatisfaction?

207. Are old ways of working, thinking, and working challenged and discussed?

208. Are people encouraged to take on new challenges that require perseverance and determination to complete?

209. Is training in your organization led by skilled insiders or outsourced to outsiders? Who decides what skills and technologies will be trained on- the people or management?

210. Do people throughout the organization have the necessary level of technical expertise and professionalism?

211. Does the organization encourage employees to reflect and share the lessons learned? Are both successes and failures shared?

212. Has the organization conducted a formal or informal exercise to understand the skills and

capabilities of their workforce critical to strategy-execution? Is there a plan to leverage strengths and remediate weaknesses?

213. Are knowledge-sharing sessions in place, or is a plan in the works to put them in place? Do leaders set the example by going first?

214. Does the organization reinforce the importance of training and upskilling and reward appropriate behaviors?

215. Is organizational-wide learning supported, encouraged, and made available?

216. Does the organization study past successes and leverage the knowledge and learnings from those events to benefit the current strategy?

217. Does the organization understand which new technologies should be learned and embraced to accelerate strategy-execution?

218. Do the right conditions exist for individuals to identify new skills required, complete the education, and test their new knowledge?

219. Do you understand which skills, technologies, and capabilities will be critical to the future, and do you have a plan for you, your team, and your organization to learn and adopt them?

220. Where do you need to improve your technical skills? What is the plan to make it happen?

221. Where do you need to improve your leadership skills? What is the plan to make it happen?

222. Where do you need to improve your coaching skills? What is the plan to make it happen?

223. What will you do to act on the above

items, and by when? How will you know if and when you are successful?

CH 8- GETTING SHIT DONE BY THINKING LIKE A LEADER

Takeaways

- Strategy and execution require different types of thinking. Strategic thinking is long-term thinking, usually in the context of 3-5 years out. Execution thinking is action-oriented thinking, focused on the present or near future.
- To close the strategy-execution gap and build operational and professional excellence in our organizations, we must act differently and think differently.
- To bridge the strategy-execution gap, a leader is also responsible for aligning the organization's primary strategy, "The Big What," to all "The Little What's" that define the daily life in the organization by integrating The How.
- Approach strategy-execution like a chess master. Never lose sight of the end objective, protect what matters, and be ready to adapt to your opponent and circumstances. Be proactive, prepared, focused, & innovative.
    - The solution that wins that game comes from studying your current opponent and making the right decisions under the present circumstances.
- The strategy-execution mindset is about making the best decision possible with the available facts and information and committing to action.
- In working to reach a decision, collaboration is essential, deliberation is vital, but there needs to be a cutoff point where people move forward in a coordinated effort. A strong leader intuitively knows where this point lies. A good decision executed quickly beats a brilliant decision implemented slowly.
- Look at execution through the lens of the Serenity Prayer-can a leader accomplish the possible, say no to the impossible, and know the difference between the two?
- Be proactive and ready to face your challenges. Being proactive means that you're prepared to act, and being

reactive means you're ready to blame. Look forward, not backward.

- Anticipate for the likely, the unlikely, and the near impossible to avoid surprises. Preparedness will improve the strength of the project.
- Be decisive. Strategy-Execution thinking isn't a lengthy process of considering your options, deliberating, thinking, discussing, pursuing one option, pulling back, deliberating further, and then doing nothing.
- Pick your battles wisely to win the war. Find the critical path through strategy-execution to deliver outstanding results in a reasonable timeframe.
- Be prepared to identify and attack the flanks of an opportunity. Use your strengths and advantages at precisely the point where your opponent or target has the most vulnerabilities.
- There is a fine line between being hailed as a maverick versus being vilified as a heretic. While execution leadership requires risk-taking and challenging the status quo in ways that shock others into a Sense of Urgency, there is a right way and a wrong way to go about it.
- Think of strategy-execution as teaching a man to fish instead of giving the man a fish. Work done should be self-sustaining and add momentum to the overall body of work, not detract from it.
- Leadership thinking isn't just about doing one thing right; it's doing many things and many different types of things, and often at the same time.

Questions

224. How many times have you been caught off guard by being unprepared? Reflect back on each scenario, consider what you could have done differently, and then consider what you must do to prepare for the next challenge.

225. Are you playing whack-a-mole to put out fires continually, or are you teaching others to fish by training others to think for themselves and create self-sustaining systems?

226. How often do you get lucky and were unprepared for the unforeseen recently? If it's often, find ways to anticipate and prepare for the unknown.

227. Do you look at work through the lens of a checkers or chess player? Do you see work as a chessboard or battlefield where your objective is to win by finding the critical path where your advantages are paired against your adversary's disadvantages?

228. Are you decisive and move quickly to address challenges, or do you wait for others to step up and do something?

229. Are you reactive or proactive? Do you make things happen, or do things happen to you?

230. Are organizational leaders trained and effective in leading others and reinforcing the strategy-execution framework?

231. As shades of grey color our environment, do you have the mental bandwidth, perspective, and experience necessary to overcome the hurdles?

232. Can you apply the spirit of the GSD body of knowledge to tackle each scenario appropriately?

233. Do you understand how to apply different

solutions to different problems?

234. Do you take the time to step back, measure yourself and your team, and adjust, or do you let yourself be consumed with busyness?

235. Do you understand when good is good enough? Do you have a methodology for identifying and claiming the highest value targets?

Maverick vs. Heretic

236. Are you bringing up problems, or are you offering to drive solutions?

237. Are you inspiring people to challenge the status quo or harassing people?

238. Are you inspiring others to embrace management's goals or objectives, or are you criticizing the administration openly?

239. Are you tone-deaf to the culture and key stakeholders while attempting to drive change while pushing people away?

240. Are you a Maverick or a Heretic in your organization? Does your view of who you match the perceptions of others?

CH 9- GETTING SHIT DONE BY EXECUTING LIKE A LEADER

Takeaways

- Leaders have power and impact that on the world around them. Leaders are vital because they can have a defining factor in many aspects of life and our world, not just historical battles.
- Whether you are working to overcome a challenging business environment, drive results on improvement projects, or even reinventing an industry in the face of new technology and competitors, success hinges on great leaders who can inspire and drive teams.
- Great leaders don't just get lucky once; they are obsessed with building an organization, a supporting team that will allow them to consistently deliver outstanding results by masterfully pairing and coordinating strategy and execution.
- On the other hand, poor leaders create other weak leaders. They poison the culture; they negate all organizational advantages and turn them into disadvantages. They keep good ideas and strategy-execution away.

241. Do your leaders have the ability to understand, prioritize, and disseminate strategy? Do your leaders have the ability, strength, and courage to challenge a bad strategy? Do they have the experience, knowledge, or capability to develop a winning strategy?

242. Do your leaders rigidly plan strategy execution, or do they give people flexibility and freedom to determine the best and most efficient execution path?

243. Do your leaders know how to identify the priorities that require the most focus? Are they capable of maintaining focus and driving resources towards that priority?

244. Do your leaders hoard responsibility for themselves, or do they share responsibility and seek out intelligent, talented, and driven people who are more knowledgeable in their areas of expertise?

245. Do your leaders take ownership of the results, good or bad? Or do they look for who to blame and punish?

246. Do your leaders communicate effectively on strategy, execution, and all the elements in between? Do your leaders listen and think before they speak?

247. Do your leaders champion and set the tone at the top to create an execution culture? Do they set an example of acceptable and unacceptable behaviors? Do they reward and punish the proper behaviors consistently?

248. Do your leaders have the right leadership behaviors? Do they set the organization in the right direction and inspire others towards action? Do they support their people when needed and remove obstacles?

249. Do your leaders have the experience to execute the strategy? Are they familiar and

knowledgeable of the elements of the strategy-execution gap, and do they have a plan to remedy each item? Do you leaders how technical and business knowledge to understand the challenges and solve them?

250. Do your leaders have the proper skills or know what skills are required to execute strategy? Are people encouraged and supported to maintain and upgrade their skills along the way?

251. Do your leaders set clear standards of professionalism to guide acceptable behaviors and expectations?

252. Do your leaders inspire and encourage a continuous improvement mindset where innovative ideas are celebrated?

253. Do your leaders champion execution? Are they focused on results and empowering people to achieve them? Do they understand the obstacles and accelerants of strategy-execution?

254. How well do you empower your organization's members to own and solve problems, distribute decision-making lower in the organizational structure, and gain from their collective knowledge?

255. How will you measure and track your progress to reach higher levels of mastery for yourself and your team?

256. Does the organization regularly discuss performance with functions/ team/individuals and share feedback? Do leaders have the courage and support they need to make adjustments?

257. Are leaders and managers trained to be authentic yet challenging?

258. Do leaders tie all of the organization's activities back to strategy-execution?

259. Is your management team engaged in executing the strategy—not just by measuring results but by constantly challenging

the organization and supporting it in improving its key capabilities?

260. What makes you the leader (why is your team inspired to follow your direction)?

261. How many of the things you do could be done by a team member?

262. Do you spend enough time and effort coaching/mentoring your team members to help them grow?

263. Do you effectively balance the big picture with technical leadership? Thinking is essential in strategy, but it isn't everything: if you don't do anything with it, it's as if it doesn't exist.

264. Are your blinders on or off? Do you make time to stop, look, and listen? Spend time working to see more and detect the opportunities missed by others. Learn to see what nobody else sees

265. What is your reputation? Are you seen as someone who drives people to be their best version?

THE KEYS TO SUCCESS

After nearly a year of thinking, reading, and writing and nearly a decade of hands-on experience, the path to closing the strategy-execution gap has flushed itself out in the below steps. If you and your organization want to Get Shit Done, you must be able and willing to check off and "own" each item.

1. Build and maintain high employee engagement levels demonstrated around ownership of Who, What, and When. Explain the Why.
2. Establish ownership in the organization. Hire the right people, trust them, and compensate them for aligning them with the organization's goals.
3. Demand high levels of professionalism by encouraging a disciplined personal development, growth, and learning structure. Through deliberate practice, encourage others to develop grit and tenacity to persevere against challenging goals. Continuous learning is a must.
4. Set Expectations of Excellence to create and maintain an environment where full accountability and excellence are the norms. A highly skilled workforce focusing on a continuous improvement mindset will beat a centralized command-and-control policy. Build Accountability Chains to increase accountability—reward excellence.
5. Ingrain a Sense of Urgency. Define the real priorities and get people and resources pointed in the right direction.
6. Acknowledge tradeoffs are required between resources. An organization must be deliberate in

choosing what to do and not do. Avoid unrealistic expectations.

7. Separate strategy-execution into two categories; the Big What and Little Whats. Individuals and teams obtain experience leading projects and improving work in their teams, departments, and functions to prepare for achieving large and complex goals.
8. Avoid static planning methodologies and embrace decentralization to allow those closest to the work to build the best solutions.
9. Set clear expectations and avoid assumptions.
10. Track and measure progress against realistic goals that have clear owners.
11. Incorporate design thinking into the Who, What, and When. Systemize and automate where possible to free time for value-added work. Remove friction wherever possible.
12. Foster excellent communication demonstrated by candor, feedback, alignment, and frequent check-ins. Be mindful in determining how we communicate to increase speed, increase accountability, and avoid confusion.
13. Build a unique and robust culture manifested through Ways of Working.
14. Minimize distractions and embrace simplicity. Focus on what matters and minimize what doesn't with the Pareto Principle.
15. Encourage individuals to learn and think like leaders and act accordingly. Encourage creativity and innovation to build systems and processes that are sustainable. Being forward-looking, prepared, and proactive are valuable characteristics. Build leadership at all levels.
16. Execute, assess, iterate. Repeat.

FINAL QUESTION:

Want more training?

- Want personal online training?
    - I have an online, multi-week course in development now.
    - Each section will share a reading list, resources, content, quizzes, and assignments. If you want to learn the habits, skills, and mindset to become a leader and Get Shit Done, this is the program for you.
- Want corporate or team training?
    - We have that, too!
    - I'm partnering with a niche consulting firm to deliver an outstanding in-person and remote program.
    - Includes everything from the individual program, workshops, and follow-up sessions to ensure the training is valued and applied.
- Please email me at Benjamin.wann1@gmail.com to register or inquire about either program.

Check out my website here:
https://benjaminwann.com/
Order Getting Shit Done here:
https://amzn.to/3dx7SFZ

www.ingramcontent.com/pod-product-compliance
Lightning Source LLC
LaVergne TN
LVHW050610100826
845148LV00015B/3201